CW00383293

Mining Communities

Miners in Belgium in the 1890s wait grimly to go underground.

WAYS OF LIFE

Mining Communities

BY BRIAN WILLIAMS

Illustrated by Tony Morris

CHERRYTREE BOOKS

Picture credits: British Coal p11, p26, p27, p44; De Beers Consolidated Mines/ Rosemary May p35 (top and bottom); Mary Evans Picture Library p2, p9; Falkirk Museum p19; Hulton Deutsch Collection p10, p24 (top), p25 (left and right); Hutchison Library p30/31, p32, p34, p39, p42, p43; Mansell Collection p18, p22, p23 (left and right); Peter Newark's American Pictures p36 (top and bottom), p37 (bottom); Zefa Picture Library p41, p45, p47.

A Cherrytree Book

Designed and produced by
AS Publishing

First published 1992
by Cherrytree Press Ltd
a subsidiary of
The Chivers Company Ltd
Windsor Bridge Road
Bath, Avon BA2 3AX

British Library Cataloguing in Publication Data
Williams, Brian
Mining Communities.—(Ways of Life Series)
I. Title II. Morris, Tony III. Series
307.7

ISBN 0-7451-5160-4

Printed and bound in Italy by L.E.G.O. s.p.a., Vicenza

Contents

Miners Together

A miner's life has traditionally been one of hardship and hazard. Mining today is easier and safer than it once was but miners the world over still share a common bond and feel a deep sense of community.

Prehistoric people picked up pebbles and flints to use as tools. In time, they learned how to dig into the ground, to mine for building stone, metals and salt.

Stone, metals, coal and many other useful substances are found in the ground. It is the work of miners to bring these precious substances to the surface. Miners need special skills and strengths to manage the difficult and dangerous tasks they undertake.

Mining began over 10,000 years ago. The first miners grubbed in the earth for stones and *flints* that they could make into tools and weapons. Later miners dug for building stone and metals such as copper, tin, iron, gold, silver and lead. They mined salt for food and coal for fuel. They pumped oil from the ground and discovered diamonds and other gems. In our own times, these substances are still mined, together with *phosphates* for fertilizers and *uranium* for nuclear power.

□Danger breeds trust

Miners and their families made their homes at places where precious *minerals* were plentiful. Over thousands of years these communities developed their own skills and customs. Because miners often lived in remote places and worked underground in darkness, their neighbours frequently regarded them with fear and awe.

Mining families stuck together, helping each other in times of trouble. And there always were troubles because mining is dangerous. With no safety devices to protect them, the earliest underground workers worked in constant fear of falling rocks and collapsing *shafts.* With no artificial lighting, they worked in darkness, relying upon each other's strength, skill and endurance. With no proper *ventilation*, they inhaled dust that damaged their lungs and made them old before their time.

□Disaster

When disaster struck an individual miner, only one family would be affected. Other members of the community would rally round to look after the miner's family. But in many disasters, the whole community would be struck, with virtually every family losing a loved-one and breadwinner.

In the face of such tragedies, miners are swift to raise money to help widows and orphans. They are even swifter to rush to the rescue of comrades in trouble.

A mine disaster. There was no shortage of volunteers to go into the smoke-filled tunnels to rescue survivors and bring out the injured and the dead.

Canaries were used to detect poisonous gas because they react to it sooner than people do.

Mine disasters live in the folk memory of every mining community. Songs are sung about the people who died, about the heroism of the rescue teams, and the sorrow of the families left to mourn.

Every mining community has its tales of heroes; of men who gave their lives for their friends. Mine accidents were often caused by neglect and bad management. Miners had to fight to win the reforms needed to make their work safer. Every disaster was a battle lost. But the mining community noted the lessons to learn, returned to work, and fought harder for change.

DISASTERS

Explosions and fires

1907 Coal mine explosion killed 361 miners at Monongha in West Virginia, USA.
1913 Electrical sparks caused an explosion of gas and coal dust that killed 439 below ground at Senghenydd, in South Wales.
1942 In the worst-ever mine explosion, 1549 miners died at the Honkeiko Colliery in China.
1956 A coal mine fire killed 262 miners at Marcinelle, Belgium.
1960 At Coalbrook in South Africa, a fire killed 437.
1965 At Bihar in India, a fire killed 375.
1972 At Wankie, Rhodesia, a coal mine explosion killed 427.
1975 At Dhanbad in India, an explosion and flood in a coal mine killed 372.
1989 Near Nazca, Peru, carbon monoxide gas killed 200 trapped gold miners.
1990 At Dobrnja, Yugoslavia, 178 died in a coal mine explosion.

Flooding

Sometimes miners accidentally broke into an old, forgotten working, filled with water seeping through the rock. Unknown numbers of miners drowned as a result.

Trapped

In one terrible accident of the 1860s the pithead machinery fell down the single shaft of a mine in Northumberland, England. The shaft was blocked by debris, and 204 men and boys were trapped. Rescuers toiled for seven days to clear a way down through the jumble of wooden beams and rubble. They found only bodies. All the trapped miners had been overcome by poisonous gas.

Avalanche

In 1966 at the village of Aberfan in South Wales a huge tip of mine waste collapsed. Tonnes of rock and mud slid down on to the village like a black avalanche. The school in its path was buried, along with 116 children. The total death toll was 144.

Every mining community shared the grief of the people of this small Welsh community. The tip was cleared, and the site landscaped to remove all traces of the disaster. Village life goes on. But the memory of that terrible day remains.

□ Together we stand

Disputes between mine owners and workers have often been long and bitter. In the past miners were often forced to work like slaves, for long hours and low wages.

They had no choice but accept the work; they needed the money and the *pit* (mine) was the only local source of income. The only way that miners could fight injustice and improve their working conditions was to band together.

Just as the miners needed the work, the mine owners needed the profits. To a certain extent, the owners were dependent on the miners. If the workers went on *strike*, their profits would fall. But if a mine closed, everyone suffered. Families lost their livelihood, and in the past this often meant that they went hungry.

A contemporary drawing of miners being killed in a gas explosion in 1892 in France.

SINGING MINERS

The *solidarity* of the mining community is often expressed in song. The feelings of the miners can be heard in the massed voices of a Welsh miners' choir or in the folk songs of the Appalachian Mountain miners of America.

□ Companies and unions

The first *unions* were formed about 200 years ago. The unions helped end such bad practices as (in America) the payment of miners in company *tokens* (instead of cash), which could only be exchanged for goods at the company store. Unions fought for better wages, shorter hours, better working conditions, and improved facilities such as bathhouses at the *pithead.*

Mining unions began as small local organizations, but have become large and powerful, particularly in the coal industry. No government wants a coal strike. So coal-mining unions enjoy considerable power in labour bargaining. Miners in one country often send money to help those on strike in another country.

□ Safety and health today

Today, mines have well-equipped rescue squads, trained for every emergency. In most countries, health and safety regulations are strictly enforced. Every effort

In cramped underground conditions miners had to depend on each other, and get along with each other.

MINING METHODS

How miners work depends on the whereabouts of the mineral they want to extract.

Strip mining

If coal seams lie just beneath the surface, the coal can be stripped away by earth movers and giant buckets on draglines. This is open-cast or *strip mining.* It is the cheapest way of getting coal out of the ground. Open-cast mining looks unsightly but when all the coal has been removed, the mine company usually puts back the soil and landscapes the area.

Drift mining

In some places a coal seam may angle down into a hillside. This happens where the rock layers or strata are bent and twisted. The coal may actually stick out of the hillside. Mining can begin at the is made to minimise dust, danger and noise and provide a safe working environment. Mineworkers are provided with training, equipment and protective clothing.

□ A better future

In the past, the mining tradition was handed, often proudly, from one generation to another. As soon as a son was old enough to work, he would go to the mine with his father. But many people dreamed of a better life, free from poverty and hardship. When education became available to the poor, many young men left mining communities to find less gruelling work and better themselves.

Today the mining industry offers opportunities for electricians, engineers, *geologists*, surveyors, salespeople, computer experts, managers, mechanics and many kinds of skilled staff, both male and female. Over a million mineworkers are employed in the United States alone.

Miners replace their lamps after a shift. *The batteries will be fully charged by the next shift.*

surface. The miners open up a tunnel and gradually work their way into the hill, following the seam deeper and deeper. This is a drift mine.

Quarrying

Many metal *ores*, such as iron, and materials such as stone and gravel are simply dug out of huge holes called *quarries*. *Sluicing* or washing the ore out with jets of water is another way of obtaining metal ores.

Underground mining

To reach coal that is deep underground, a long shaft must first be dug from the surface. *Galleries* or tunnels extend either side of the shaft into the coal *seams*. On the surface is the *winding gear*, which raises and lowers the elevator-like *cage* that carries the miners up and down the shaft, and the coal from the mine.

Once all coal-cutting was done by hand. As the coal was removed, the tunnel roof was supported with wooden props or by leaving pillars of coal. Today huge machines cut coal and load it on to conveyors, propping the tunnel with steel roof supports. Lasers guide the tunnellers so that they cut and blast tunnels in exactly the right spot. Fans blow fresh air through the mine. Water sprays keep down the dust and refrigeration units keep the mine cool. Many mines are very extensive, and some miners travel 10 kilometres or so underground each time they go to work.

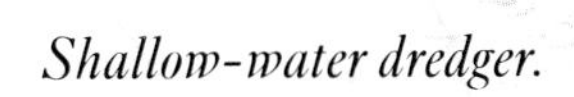

Shallow-water dredger.

Dredging

Mineral deposits at the bottom of a shallow lake or river can be scooped up by a floating dredger, a ship with an endless chain of buckets.

Pumping

Some lakes and seas contain huge amounts of mineral elements. The water is pumped into treatment plants and the minerals are separated from it.

Miners of Long Ago

Mining was crucial to the development of civilization. The use of metals to make tools enabled farmers to work the land, and the use of metals to make weapons enabled them to protect themselves and their possessions.

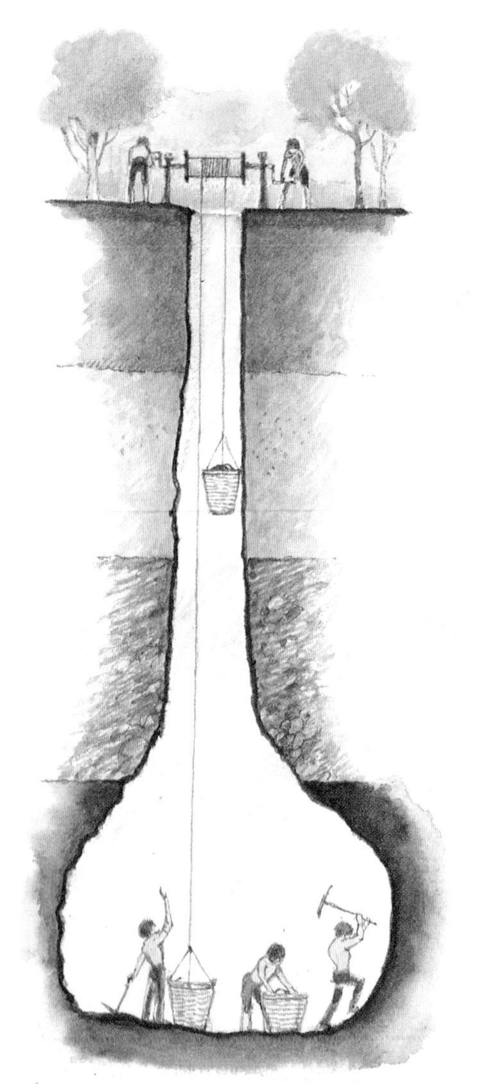

Learning to make and use tools and fire were important steps in the evolution of human beings. The first tools were simply pieces of flint and rock found on the ground. As prehistoric people realised the usefulness of certain shapes, they chipped away at the flints to make shapes that were good for cutting, scraping or piercing. More and more flint was needed but reaching it and digging it from the rocks was difficult – with only flint itself and tools made from antlers and bones to hack away at the rock.

□ Flint miners

Flint miners dug *bellpits*. These were holes, or shafts, up to 10 metres deep, with a bell-shaped chamber at the bottom. The miners hacked away at the sides until the pit began to collapse. Then they abandoned it and moved on.

Evidence of pits, dug about 4000 years ago, have been found at several sites in Europe. The miners cut galleries, or tunnels, outwards from a central shaft, leaving pillars of rock to support the roof. Working by the flickering light of animal-fat lamps, they must have had considerable courage, strength and skill. They had no *explosives*, so they cracked rocks with fire, followed by a dousing of water. They climbed down into the darkness on a ladder made from a tree branch, or were lowered dangling on the end of a rope.

Prehistoric salt miners at work. The men hacked away the salt in lumps and carried it out of the mine. Women hammered the lumps into smaller pieces. Salt was a valuable trade item, so mining it was worth the effort.

The miners passed knowledge of the skills they acquired from generation to generation. They mined for only part of the year. The rest of the time they looked after their crops and animals. They kept some of the flints they mined for themselves, and traded the rest for other goods, such as salt.

□ Salt miners

Salt has been important since the earliest times, for seasoning and preserving food. It was highly prized in all early civilizations. Small amounts could be got from the sea and some was found on the surface, but in other places it was deep underground. The Romans built the *Via Salaria* (Salt Road) between Rome and the port of Ostia where there was a saltworks that dried sea salt.

In China, there were salt mines 600 metres deep. In 100BC, the emperor *nationalized* all the mines. The miners worked in appalling conditions and were little more than slaves. But salt was big business, and was carried by road all the way from China to the West.

Opposite page: A bellpit in operation in medieval times. Before pulleys were invented, miners had to carry their loads up the rope.

□ Ancient metalworkers

The first metals to be dug out of the ground were copper and gold. This was more than 5000 years ago in the Middle East. The first miners were the first metal-workers as well. They were the supreme technologists of their time.

Copper is a fairly soft metal, but when combined with tin it makes the *alloy* bronze which is much stronger. Bronze was used as early as 3000BC in Mesopotamia. In most places, it was superseded by iron which was plentiful, but difficult to extract from the ores (metal-bearing rocks) in which it was found.

Iron ore has to be heated to a very high temperature to separate the metal from the rock. When people learned how to *smelt* iron in this way, the Iron Age began – at different times in different places. Even when separated, iron was not molten enough to be shaped. It had to be reheated and hammered and reheated and hammered. But when the work was done, the iron was strong. The Hittites, Chinese, Greeks and Indians all mastered the secret of iron-making, surrounding the mysterious science with ritual and magic.

□ The mining might of Rome

The Romans knew that there was power and wealth in mining. In every territory they conquered they took over the mines and ran them like a military operation. Miners in Ancient Rome were mostly slaves, at the bottom of society. They worked up to 200 metres below ground, often in terrible conditions. Few lived to see old age. Deep mines were subject to rock falls and flooding. Waterwheels were sometimes used to raise water from mines. But more often slaves with buckets did the job.

MINING IN THE MIDDLE AGES

During the Middle Ages miners began using *gunpowder* to crack open rocks. In Britain coal mining began as early as 1210. The monks of Newbottle Abbey, in Lancashire, had a *charter* granting them the right to dig coal. But many people were frightened by the thick black smoke and strong smell that came from the burning mineral. In 1306 the burning of coal was banned, but later the ban was lifted as the value of coal became apparent. Coal from the north east was brought to London in ships; it was known as 'seacoal'. The other main European coal-mining regions were Belgium and Germany.

By late medieval times, the miner had become a person of importance. In Germany, miners did not have

Iron miners smelted the ore they cut from the rocks in charcoal ovens. The man on the right is using bellows to blow air into the oven, to raise the temperature inside. The heat melted the iron ore into a workable lump which cooled after the oven was broken open (left) with a pickaxe. *The iron was then hammered and reheated to shape it.*

to serve in the army, like other workers, and did not pay taxes. Miners were free to *prospect,* or look for, precious metals, more or less where they liked. They even had their own courts and parliaments. Miners formed small groups called associations to protect their privileges.

Miners lost these privileges as their industry grew. Deeper mines needed equipment such as pumps, and small associations could not afford them. Mines were bought up by wealthy landowners and merchants, and the miners were paid wages instead of running their own mines. For many miners, this was to lead to hard times.

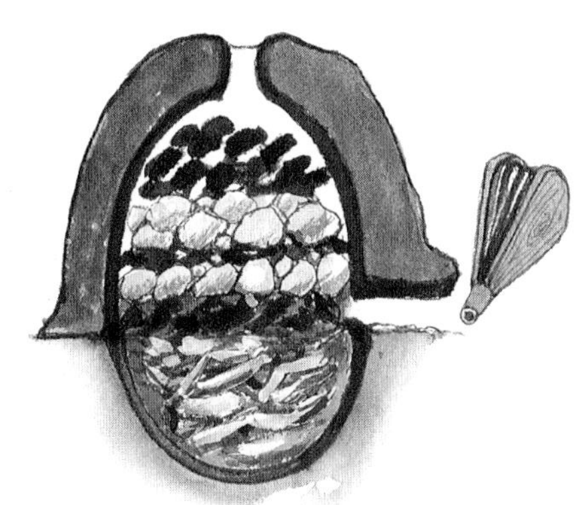

Inside an oven.

The raw materials needed to make glass are sand, soda ash and limestone and strong heat. Glass-blowing was invented by the Syrians about 2000 years ago. In America, glass was first made in Mexico in the 1500s. Coal was used for making glass from medieval times.

MINERS OF THE NEW WORLD

Long before the first Europeans reached America, the people there had discovered and learned how to use many minerals. The Aztec people of Mexico and the Incas of Peru picked up gold specks from fast-flowing streams. They did not need to tunnel underground, for all the gold they needed was easily found. There was silver, too, especially in the silver mines of Potosi in Bolivia, which the Spanish *conquistadors* discovered in the 1540s.

□ Gold greed

The Europeans were greedy for gold and silver, and ruthlessly pillaged the Indians' treasure. They melted down gold ornaments and jewellery and shipped gold bars back to Spain. They forced the Indians to work as slaves in underground mines. So much gold and silver was shipped to Europe from America that many European gold and silver miners lost their jobs.

The Spanish soldiers destroyed the Aztec and Inca empires. Many Indians were killed, or died from disease, and their way of life was wiped out. Few Europeans made any effort to understand or preserve the culture of

Pueblo Indians making pots. These Americans knew how to build coal-burning kilns *in which to fire their clay pots to harden them.*

the Indians. Lured on by false tales of a mythical land called El Dorado, overflowing with treasure, they were desperate to find more gold.

□ Miners of North America

North America was also rich in minerals though it is not known how much these were exploited by the original inhabitants. Pueblo Indians of the south-western United States burned coal in pottery kilns and the Navaho made beautiful silver jewellery, with skills probably learned from the people of Mexico.

The European settlement of North America affected many miners. Coal mining by settlers began in the 1700s in Virginia and Pennsylvania, and more and more minerals were found. Some mines in Europe could not compete with the New World's cheap copper, tin and lead and had to close. Rich *reserves* of copper were found on the Keewenaw peninsula in Michigan, where mining began in 1844. Later in the 1800s miners moved into western states including Nevada and Montana. Chile in South America also became a copper mining region.

Later still, gold was found, and in the 1800s thousands flocked to gold mining areas in pursuit of instant wealth.

THE INDUSTRIAL REVOLUTION

Life for small mining communities changed for ever with the Industrial Revolution of the 1700s. Steam power and the *mass-production* of iron needed coal, and to mine the coal more and more workers were needed. People who had never been underground in their lives went to work in the new mines.

Steel is an alloy of iron, and is even stronger. Because it was difficult to make it was regarded as a semi-precious metal. In the 1850s a new technique was invented that allowed steel to be made cheaply and easily from kinds of ore that were abundant in Europe and North America. Iron production declined and steel superseded it completely. It was used for making railways, ships, bridges, towers, tools and canned foods. The United States and Germany became the largest producers.

The ironworks at Coalbrookdale in Shropshire, England. Here Abraham Darby in 1708 first smelted ironstone with coke *made from mined coal. Coalbrookdale became England's greatest iron-producing centre.*

The discovery of electricity brought a new source of power to industry and to people's homes. Electricity could be made from coal and also from oil, which largely replaced coal as a power source for industry and transport. Today, much electricity is produced by *nuclear power* – which depends on uranium, a rare metal that is mined in very small quantities but generates huge amounts of energy.

TIN MINERS

Tin was mined for over 2000 years in Cornwall, the most westerly county in England. The Cornish tinners were proud and independent. In the Middle Ages they were free from many of the laws applied to other citizens. They had their own law courts, called the stannary courts. These Cornish miners were masters of rock craft and skilled engineers. They took their skills all over the world, especially during the 1800s when the Cornish industry fell on hard times. The shallow tin mines became exhausted, and many miners left home for good, travelling by ship to America and Australia.

The Coal Miners

Coal has been burned as fuel since prehistoric times. Communities with coal deposits grew rich, especially during the Industrial Revolution, but the people who physically dug out the coal often benefited least from the riches they mined.

Son followed father and grandfather into the pit. These five Scottish miners of the early 1900s represent three generations of one family of colliers.

To most people, miners are coal miners. Today coal is challenged by other *fossil fuels*, such as natural gas and oil, which are more convenient to use, but the world has more plentiful coal *deposits.* Coal will provide the world with energy for many years to come. There is enough coal to last 200 years, long after natural gas and oil supplies have been used up – if we go on using them at the present rate.

The United States is the world's leading exporter of coal, and has about a third of the world's coal reserves. Next come Russia and China. Europe, Canada, Australia, India and South Africa are also major coal producers.

A mining village was a small, close-knit community. The winding gear at the pithead loomed over the little houses and was a daily reminder that everyone owed their livelihoods to the mine and the mine-owners.

□ The Industrial Revolution

By the 1800s 'coal was king'. Coal fired the pounding steam engines in factories and provided the coke for *blast furnaces* making steel. Miners helped fuel the new Industrial Revolution. More and more were needed, as new mines were dug. Coal near the surface, easily mined, was quickly used up, and the new mines were often very deep. Many mine owners were interested in profits, not safety. Wages were low. The men worked long hours, in terrible conditions, amid choking dust and dripping water.

□ Going underground

The miners' working day began with the descent into the mine. They stepped into a cage, a kind of wire-sided lift that carried them down the mineshaft. As the gates clanged shut, the winding machinery above hummed into action. The cage, hung from strong cables, dropped down into the darkness of the subterranean world.

A modern mine is well lit and ventilated with fresh air. It was very different in the past. Small boys aged 6 to 10 worked as *trappers*. They were in charge of the doors that controlled the flow of air through the tunnels. They sat in the darkness for hours, with no one to talk to.

□ Dangerous gases

The use of naked lights often caused explosions of dangerous gases, until *safety lamps* were invented in the early 1800s. Later electricity came into the mines, banishing the darkness. In an emergency, miners used to take caged canaries down the mine with them. The birds reacted very quickly if they breathed in dangerous gases. If a bird became unconscious, the miners would hurry to safety – usually in plenty of time to revive the canary in fresh air. Nowadays specially trained rescue teams use sophisticated electronic gas detectors.

□ Hacking and hewing

In some mines, the seams (layers of coal) were so narrow that men worked on their knees or lying on their sides. Their backs were cut and bruised by the surrounding

This nineteenth-century illustration shows the tasks assigned to women and children in the mines. It does not show the narrowness of the tunnels or the choking dust and dirt.

rock as they hacked at the coal with picks. Coal cutting machines were first used in the 1860s, and were adopted much faster in American mines than in the deeper mines of Europe. *Mechanization* increased production. It also made working underground easier.

The king of the underground workers was the *hewer* – the man with the pick who worked at the coal face. He needed not just enormous physical strength, but also a kind of sixth sense to warn him of possible danger. While he was young and strong, a man could earn good money. But as he grew older, he was usually moved to lower-paid surface work. In old age (and in the 1800s anyone over 40 was considered elderly) a man might be found working among women and children surface-workers, shamefacedly picking out stones and other rubbish from the coal.

Until this century, men worked extremely long shifts. Even in the United States, 60 hours was the normal working week until 1898. Today, most miners in western countries work up to 35 hours a week with two days off.

Above left: Miners descending the shaft were packed into cages like sardines in a tin

Above right: Boys sorting usable coal from unusable lumps of rock. Surface work was safer but less well-paid.

□ Pit women and children

Today, women have won the right to work underground in mines, almost 150 years after they had been banned from such work because of the dreadful hardship it imposed on them. In the early 1800s in Europe, women and children worked underground in conditions that would shock us today. They were treated worse than the *pit ponies*. Women carried heavy baskets of coal on their backs or pulled small coal wagons. Harnessed to the wagons, they scrambled along tunnels on hands and knees. Their ragged clothes were soaked by water dripping from the roof, and their skin was rubbed red raw by the chafing straps and chains of the harness.

Women worked 12-hour shifts in these appalling conditions, and still had to look after their homes. Not until 1842 did the British government ban women and children (girls and boys under the age of 10) from working underground. Children aged 12 still worked in the mines until 1882. Canada and the United States, and most other western countries introduced similar bans, but in some third world countries today, there are no laws to prevent the use of child *labour* in mines.

□ Home and family

Miners' families have always shared the hardships of mining life. Looking after the home on a very small income and with no modern *amenities* was very hard work in itself. Women in mining villages were up early. A *knocker-up*, usually a retired miner, went from house to house, to rouse the miners working the early shift. A miner's wife might be up at 2.30 in the morning, with a long day ahead.

Everyone knew that even the strongest men would be weary when work was finished. Most miners lived close to the mine. In the 1800s many mine communities had no shops, schools or hospitals. Men walked home from the pit, clothes black with coal dust, their skin scarred and grimy. There were no mine baths. Mothers, wives and children waited for their menfolk to return. They prepared hot food, a bath in front of the fire, and clean clothes.

Not a moment to waste, this women does her crochet work while carrying a huge load of coal. Coal was burned on open fires in British homes until pollution *control laws were enacted in the 1950s.*

□ Women's work

There were always filthy clothes for the women to wash by hand. Miners' homes in the old days had no running water. The women carried water in buckets from a pump outside. In winter, wet clothes dripped and steamed in the kitchen.

Often a family took in a single miner as a lodger. This brought more money into the home, but also more washing and more meals to cook. Girls helped their mothers with the chores. They heated bathwater, washed clothes, greased boots, scrubbed wooden tables, baked bread, did the shopping, cared for sick babies. Sometimes women turned their front rooms into shops, selling bacon (many miners kept pigs) or eggs. The extra money was welcome.

COAL POWER

So vital was coal during World War II (1939-45) that in Britain 20,000 young men were drafted into the coal mines.

In 1984 Britain had its worst-ever miners' strike. It lasted a year. Mining communities were torn apart. In the end, the miners lost, and more mines were closed. Since that time 100 mines have closed and 139,000 jobs have been shed.

Striking coal miners in Russia and Romania played a significant part in the social upheavals that accompanied the ending of communist rule in Eastern Europe.

□ A man's life

On their day off, some men went to church. For others, drink and gambling blotted out their aches and pains, and helped them forget the dangers underground. Miners lived by a tough code of rules. Outsiders feared them as lawless and violent, and some miners were indeed hard-fighting and hard-drinking. They had their own punishments for wrongdoing. In the early 1800s miners sometimes beat child-workers who broke the rules underground. The theft of a man's dinner was punished by a severe beating with wooden sticks. These punishments were sometimes so shocking that local law courts took action against the miners.

Right: July 1912: miners and their families watch reverently as bodies are removed from Cadeby Colliery in Yorkshire. An explosion killed 35 miners, a second blast killed 53 rescuers.

Below: A coal heaver (deliveryman) acting as a picket *in support of striking miners in 1921. Coal heavers wore leather hats with a flap to protect their shoulders.*

□ Communities in sorrow

Rock falls, explosions and floods often occurred, without warning, and caused dreadful loss of life in mines that were unsafe. Miners and their families faced these tragedies courageously. The mine was their only means of support, so surviving miners had to go back to work for their own sake, and for the sake of the families of their dead or injured comrades.

Today, *compensation* is paid to those suffering ill-health or hardship, but in the past it was up to the miners themselves to help each other. The sense of comradeship amongst coal-mining communities, and with their fellows in far-off places, is deep. If a mining community suffers a tragedy or strike, financial assistance is swift to arrive. Fortunately disasters are rare today, but miners' solidarity is as strong as ever.

In a modern mine, tunnelling machines, like huge corkscrews, cut through the rock to reach fresh seams of coal.

□Fathers and sons

In many mining areas, the pit was virtually the only source of jobs. A boy could find work in the mine, go hungry or move elsewhere. Despite dreams of a better future, sons frequently followed fathers into the mine, and they often worked side by side. When times were bad, there was no work. In the days before modern wage agreements and *welfare insurance* that meant hungry families and people scavenging on waste tips for coal to burn on their fires.

A few miners' sons did leave home, to find work in other towns. But most boys went down the pit as soon as they left school. If a mine closed, miners and their families would move to a neighbouring mine. If all the local mines closed, they had to move further afield. In the late 1800s many miners left Europe for new lives in America and Australia.

□ Coal mining today

In modern times, coal miners in the West have enjoyed rising standards of living. But rival fuels such as oil and natural gas threaten old, inefficient mines. When their mines are threatened with closure, miners fight a losing battle to defend their communities.

In 1914 nine out of ten British warships burned coal mined from the Rhondda valley in South Wales. In 1990 the last mine in the valley closed. The Rhondda's green fields and woodland became a mining area in the late 1800s. People came from all over Britain to work there. There were once more than 50 mines. Nearly everyone in South Wales worked in the mines, or was related to someone who did.

Miners ride to work on quiet, clean underground trains. Sometimes the coalface is as far as 10 kilometres from the pithead.

□ Farewell to the old ways

When the mines closed, some people moved away to look for new jobs. Others stayed in the mining villages, but without jobs or in jobs specially created with government help. They looked back on the old times with nostalgia. Miners admitted that the work was hard and dirty, and sometimes crippling. Yet they also remembered the humour and comradeship of underground life.

That old way of life is fast vanishing all over the world as mining becomes a *high-tech* machine industry. Miners have become technicians. There are now fewer mines, but they produce more coal. Today an American miner can produce about 20 tonnes of coal a day, three times as much as in 1950.

These improvements have been brought about by mechanization. Machines now mine coal once too deep or difficult to reach. Strip (open-cast) mining, which requires fewer workers, is more widespread. Many strip miners do not belong to traditional miners' unions and do not live in traditional mining communities.

In the future, sons will no longer follow fathers into the pit. The world will still need coal and coalminers. But the miners of the next century will create new and different traditions for themselves.

Minerals Around the World

North America
North America is rich in minerals. It has enormous amounts of copper, crude oil, lead and coal, as well as iron ore. It also consumes a lot, and some reserves are becoming exhausted. There are large coal fields in the east, in the central region and in the Rocky Mountains. Other minerals found in North America include gold, silver, nickel, zinc, titanium, tungsten and uranium. Recently diamonds have been found in Canada.

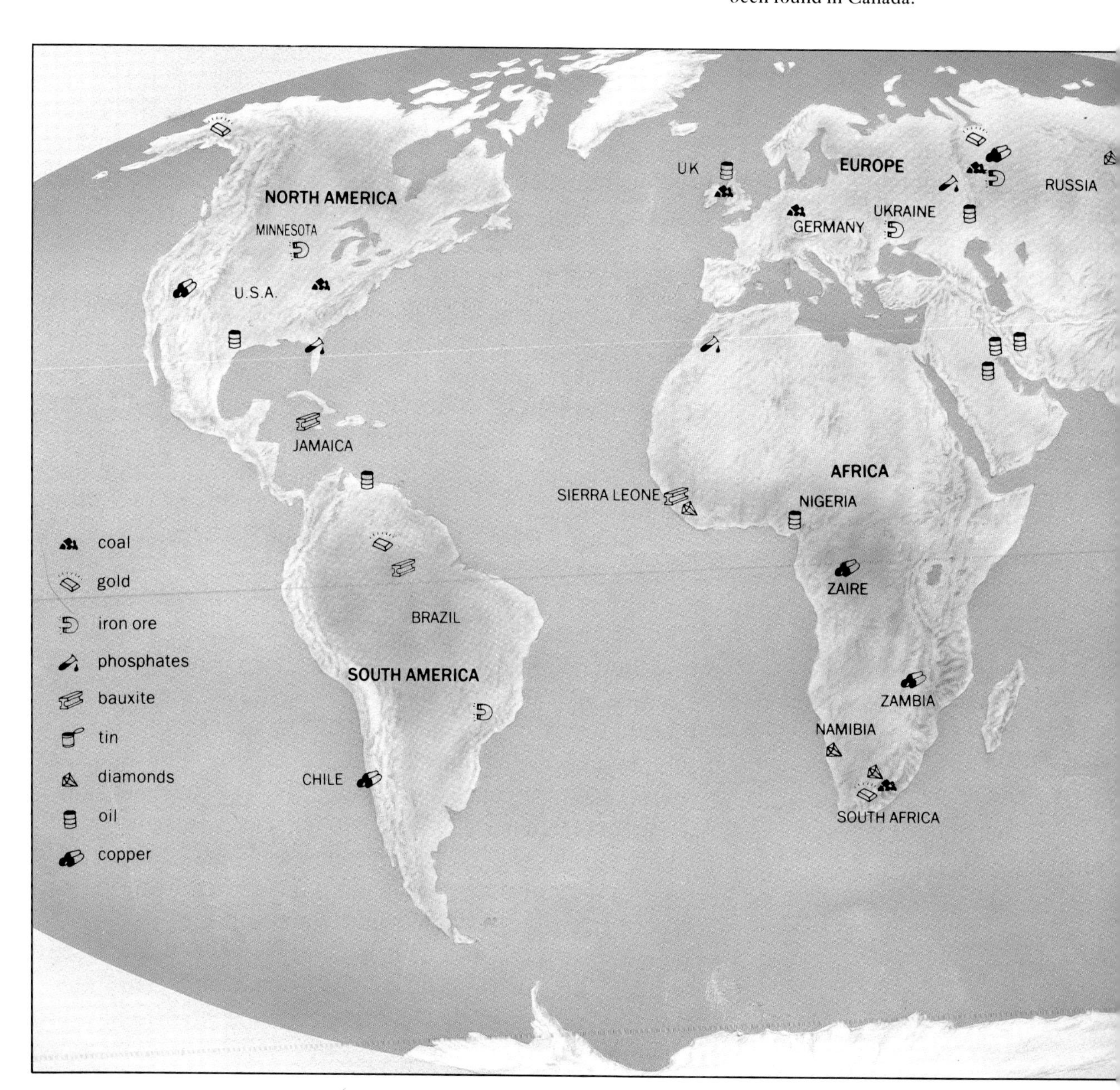

North America produces one-third of the world's phosphates and potash, which are used to make fertilizer.

Most of North America's petroleum and natural gas come from the Great Plains area, from Alaska and from beneath the sea in the Gulf of Mexico.

Jamaica, in the Caribbean, is a major source of bauxite ore, from which aluminium is made.

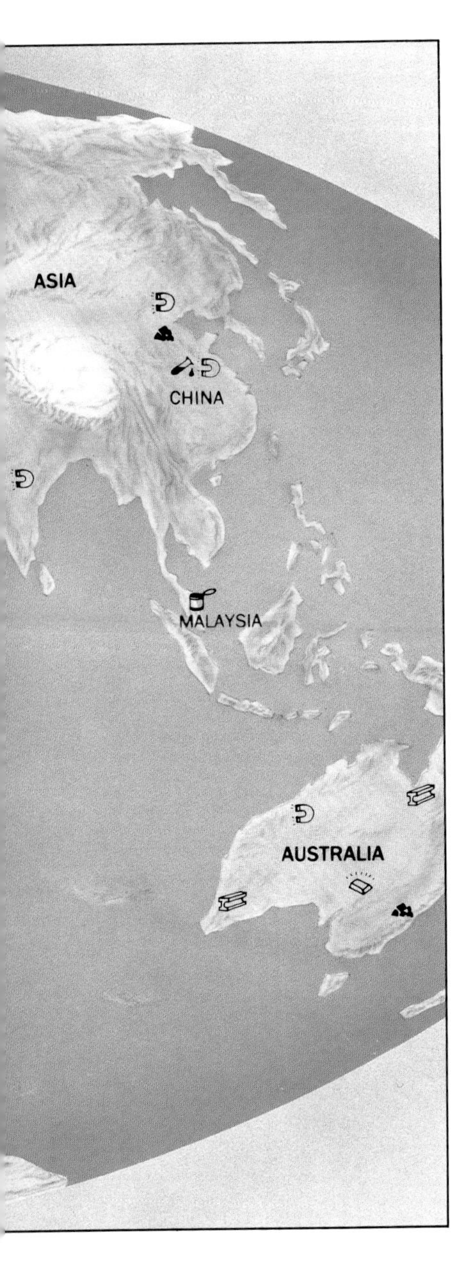

Europe

Europe has a wide variety of minerals and mining has been important there since ancient times. Europe is especially rich in coal, iron ore, natural gas and petroleum. There are big coal fields in the United Kingdom, Germany, France, Poland, Russia and Ukraine. Sweden and Russia have iron mines. Norway, the United Kingdom and the Netherlands pump oil and gas from deposits beneath the North Sea.

Most of Europe's minerals are mined in the north and centre of the continent. The southern Mediterranean region has fewer minerals. Ukraine and Russia are the leading mining countries of the former Soviet Union. Their mines produce coal, gold, iron ore, copper, manganese, nickel, platinum and diamonds.

Europe's mineral wealth helped begin the Industrial Revolution in the 1700s. Britain's coal mines, for example, fed the factories with fuel for their steam engines. Minerals were the raw materials for the new industries.

Africa

North Africa, especially Libya and Algeria, is rich in oil. Nigeria is the biggest African oil producer south of the Sahara. Other important mining countries are Zaire and Zambia (copper and cobalt), Guinea (bauxite) and South Africa. South Africa has large coal reserves and is the world's biggest producer of gold. It also produces diamonds, chromium, manganese and platinum. Diamonds are also mined in Sierrra Leone, Ghana and Namibia.

The map shows some of the places where large deposits of minerals have been found.

South America

Brazil, Chile and Venezuela are the South American countries with most minerals. Brazil has oil, iron ore, manganese, bauxite, niobium and gold. Chile produces copper and sodium nitrate, used to make fertilizer. Venezuela is South America's foremost oil producer. Colombia, as well as having coal, lead, copper and zinc mines, also produces many of the world's finest emeralds.

Asia

Southwest Asia (including Saudi Arabia, the Gulf states, Iraq and Iran) is an important oil-producing region. The Middle East has more than half of the world's oil. Saudi Arabia is second only to Russia as an oil producer. Asia is also rich in other minerals. Southeast Asia (Malaysia) is an important source of tin. India has coal, chromium, iron ore and manganese. China has a wealth of minerals including iron ore, coal, lead, tungsten, mercury and gold. Japan has coal, copper, lead, limestone, manganese, silver, tin and zinc, but only in small quantities. It has to import most of its mineral raw materials, and also the oil and coal its industries burn as fuel.

Australasia

Australia is a very important mining country. It is the leading world producer of bauxite, diamonds and lead, and Australian mines also produce coal, copper, gold, iron ore, manganese, nickel, silver, tin, titanium, tungsten and zinc. Australia had its own gold rush in the 1850s. There is natural gas and oil in the waters offshore. Australia also has the world's largest reserves of uranium.

Mining Metals

The ability to extract metals and transform them into tools and weapons gave prehistoric peoples an advantage over their neighbours. Even today the richest countries are those that exploit their natural mineral wealth.

In 1922 archaeologists found masses of gold and jewels inside the tomb of the Ancient Egyptian boy-king Tutankhamun, who died about 1352 BC. But there was only one knife and a bracelet made of iron. Iron was probably then more valuable even than gold. Yet iron is a common metal; only aluminium is more plentiful on Earth.

Copper, gold and silver occur in almost pure form and are so soft that they can be shaped without heat. Small amounts of tin heated with copper form bronze, an alloy that was easy for primitive people to shape into weapons, tools, bowls and even decorative objects. Iron is difficult to extract, but once people had learned how to smelt the iron, they could take advantage of its great strength.

Iron and its alloy steel have been the most important metals in use since it was first discovered, with the result that the world is running short of the high-grade ores needed for making the vast amounts of steel that are used today in the construction, automobile, aircraft, weapons and other manufacturing industries.

IRON MINERS

Today there are iron mining communities in Ukraine (the world leader in iron ore production), Brazil, Australia, China, India and Sweden. In the United States the chief iron ore states are Minnesota and Michigan. In Venezuela, South America, there is a mountain of iron, called Cerro Bolivar.

Even a relatively small open-cast mine destroys the landscape. Some are like huge canyons, 150 metres deep and stretching for several kilometres.

□Minnesota miners

The Minnesota iron industry began in the 1880s when settlers began mining in the Vermilion Range. Life for the miners was hard and dangerous. Dust made their health deteriorate and few avoided injuries from rock

falls. Weary from the hard physical labour, many miners spent their leisure hours in bars, though drinking was frowned upon in many communities.

Miners came to Minnesota from Germany, Sweden, Norway and other parts of Europe. They worked first with picks and shovels, and then with drills and explosives. Iron was shipped to the port of Duluth on Lake Superior, and on to the steelmaking city of Pittsburgh. In the 1890s machines moved in, as giant steam shovels took over the work. During the economic depression of the 1930s, many miners lost their jobs as the demand for steel declined.

Today, Minnesota's mining communities produce about 70 per cent of America's iron ore, even though the best ore has been used up. The mines look like enormous gashes in the earth, cut into ridges by the great crawling machines. Nowadays there are no gangs of men with picks, just huge trains and trucks carrying ore to the treatment plant. Though there are fewer of them than in the past, the workers are well treated and enjoy a high standard of living.

With the decline in the quality and, as a result, the demand for its ore, many of Minnesota's iron ore miners have had to switch to other jobs. Even more people in the steelmaking industry, in the United States, Canada, Britain and other western countries, have lost their jobs as the industry has declined.

Above: In Zambia's copper belt, miners and their families live in purpose-built townships close to the mine.

MINERS OF THE FAR NORTH

Many minerals are found in the Arctic. Miners in the far north of Canada, Alaska, Russia and Scandinavia lead an extraordinary life. During the winter months it is often so cold that work has to stop because even the equipment is frozen solid. Winter days last only a few hours, so even surface work has to be carried out under artificial lighting.

In Russia, miners are now hoping for more comforts. They used to be perpetually cold, ill-fed and ill-housed in villages that were like work camps. In Sweden, the Arctic miners live in relative luxury. The mining company provides warm workclothes, apartments, shops, cinemas and leisure centres.

Right: Malaysian tin miners. Men and women work with pans to separate granules of tin from gravel washed along the sluices.

MINING IN AFRICA AND ASIA

The modern world needs vast amounts of copper, tin and bauxite (the ore from which aluminium is obtained). These minerals can mostly be mined more cheaply in less developed countries where *labour costs* are low. Miners work long hours for low wages. The minerals they extract are mostly exported to feed the industries of the more *developed nations.*

Copper is an excellent *conductor* of electricity and heat, and is widely used in the electricity industry, and in *electroplating* and for boilers. It makes many alloys, chiefly bronze (with tin), brass (with zinc) and cupro-nickel (with nickel). Tin is soft and hardly *tarnishes.* It is mostly used to plate thin steel for making into tin cans. Aluminium is light and strong. It is made into wire, aircraft, pots and pans, and kitchen foil.

□ Malaysia tin miners

Malaysia is the world's leading producer of tin. Some ore is extracted by washing it out of the earth using a powerful water jet. The *slurry* (rock and water mixed)

Bauxite mining in Jamaica. The ore is scooped up by diggers and carted away in trucks for processing.

runs into long channels or sluices. Men and women work in the hot sun, with pans, to separate the heavier tin ore from the gravel.

Mining has brought a new way of life to many Malaysians. People whose grandparents were farmers or fishermen now work in the tin mines. The money Malaysia earns from selling tin helps to pay for schools, hospitals and roads.

□ People of the copper belt

Some countries depend heavily on mining. Zambia in central Africa earns 80 per cent of its export income from copper. The mining area is called the copper belt. Mining began in the 1920s when Zambia was part of the British empire. African peasant farmers were recruited to work in the mines, leaving their villages and learning mining skills.

Today, Zambians help run their mining industry, even though the mines are owned by international companies. If the price of copper falls, countries like Zambia suffer, and the communities that depend on miners' wages suffer too.

Zambia's neighbour Zaire also depends on mining. Both countries *export* cobalt which is used to make light alloys for jet engines and other industrial uses. The United States *imports* a third of the world's cobalt because its own reserves are no longer worth mining.

METEORITES

Not all iron comes from the Earth. The iron that prehistoric people found and used to make tools probably came from space. The bits of iron were probably from meteorites that broke up on impact with the ground, scattering pieces in all directions.

UNDERSEA MINING

Many minerals are washed into the sea by rivers. Dredgers scoop up gravel in shallow offshore waters. Special dredgers are now used to lift manganese nodules from the sea bed, 3000 metres below the surface. The nodules contain valuable amounts of copper, nickel and cobalt.

MINERS OF THE CARIBBEAN

Jamaica is the world's leading producer of bauxite. This clay-like mineral is turned into aluminium, one of the most useful of all metals. The bauxite industry began in the 1950s in Jamaica, bringing new mining and processing jobs to the island's people.

Formerly, most people had worked in agriculture, producing sugar, coffee, bananas and other fruit, but many were unemployed and emigrated to find jobs elsewhere, particularly in Britain. Because of the great natural beauty of the island and its sunny climate, Jamaica also attracts many tourists who see little of the huge strip mines and the great furnaces in which the bauxite is smelted.

Gold and Diamonds

Rare and precious, gold has been the most sought-after metal for thousands of years. Many lives and fortunes have been lost in the pursuit of it. Many of those who mine it today have no chance of owning more than a speck of it.

Rough diamonds (above) are cut and polished so that they sparkle brilliantly.

Gold does not tarnish and grow dull. It can be easily shaped into ornaments and jewels that will never lose their lustre. Mines over three kilometres deep have been dug to find it. Gold *ingots*, worth billions and billions of pounds, are hidden below ground in high-security vaults. Money is still valued by its worth in gold. Governments of those nations that possess gold strictly supervise the mining of it. South Africa, Russia, Canada, the United States, Australia and Ghana have the world's largest gold deposits.

Other precious metals include silver and platinum. Like gold, these are used industrially as well as for jewellery. Even more rare and expensive are a few recently discovered metals, such as titanium, tantalum, vanadium and a series of platinum-like metals, which are used in the manufacture of military and space equipment.

□ Gold rushes

Gold has been mined, admired, hoarded and traded since prehistoric times. Wherever gold is discovered hopeful people flock. In the 1800s thousands of people travelled to America, Canada, South Africa and Australia dreaming of getting rich by finding gold. Few knew much about mining, but they set off into the wilderness with high hopes. Mining camps sprang up overnight. Some grew into cities. Many more vanished, almost as rapidly as they had appeared.

□Great California Gold Rush

In January 1848 gold was discovered on the American River in California. By spring the whole country from San Francisco to the Sierra Nevada mountains rang with the excitement of a gold rush. Farmers left their fields half-planted, houses were left empty. Everyone bought a shovel and a pickaxe and headed for the goldfields.

The first arrivals were lucky. Some made fortunes. A day's work could yield an ounce of gold, worth about 20 dollars (20 times a workman's daily wage). San Francisco, then a port with only 2000 inhabitants, became the magnet for prospectors arriving by sea. There was no railway across America, so people from the eastern states faced a long sea voyage around South America. Some struggled overland through the swamps and jungles of Panama, while others set out to cross the great plains and mountains of the American wilderness.

Above: Heading west and hopeful. People travelled to California by whatever means they could, but crowded on to ill-equipped wagons, many died before they reached California.

Right: Mining camps grew at an astonishing rate. Soon wooden buildings replaced the tents and shacks of the first arrivals.

□Murder and misery

The first arrivals seized the best *claims.* Latecomers set up camp where they could. The men lived in rough wooden shacks, but often slept in tents to guard their claims. Settlements grew into towns, but with no town government and no law and order. Miners fought and killed one another. Traders moved in to sell tools, clothing and food. The miners lived on a monotonous diet of pork, beans and bread. They sickened with dysentery and scurvy, and there were often outbreaks of deadly diseases such as cholera and typhus.

When they were not working their claims, gold miners drank and gambled in the squalid saloons that sprouted like mushrooms in the camps. In some *gold-strike* towns, every third cabin was a saloon. The women who came with the saloon-keepers were as tough as the men. On Sundays, work stopped. There were horse races, prize fights and other amusements to attract crowds – and relieve miners of their hard-earned dollars. James Marshall, the man who first found the gold, died a poor man. So did most of the 'Forty-Niners'. Very few found the fortune for which they had suffered such hardships.

Above: Panning *for gold was the cheapest way to look for it. All you needed was a shallow metal pan, a stretch of river and keen eyes.*

Left: 'Sunday morning in the mines'. In this painting, the miners relax. Some, sober and hopeful, read or write or do their washing. Others despair or drown their sorrows with drink. The wisest head for home.

□ Ghost towns and new communities

Similar gold rushes took place in Australia (in 1851), in South Africa (in 1886) and in Canada (in 1897). By the early 1900s the lone gold prospector was rare. Mining companies moved in to buy up the best claims. Unlucky miners moved on. They left behind *ghost towns* of empty buildings and silent streets. Some ghost towns remain. Others have been taken over by farmers.

□Miners of Brazil

Today, in the Amazon region of Brazil, gold miners are again journeying into the wilderness. Many leave their families in distant villages. The mines are huge holes in which men toil like mud-sodden ants, struggling under the weight of sacks of ore which may contain a grain or two of precious gold.

OTHER GOLD RUSHES

Alaska
Alaska had been the setting off point for thousands of hopeful prospectors making their way to the Yukon in 1897 and 1898. In 1899 gold was discovered at Nome and the miners flocked there. More gold was found at Fairbanks in 1903.

Australia
In 1850 gold was discovered in New South Wales, Australia. People rushed from Melbourne, the nearest large town. Streets were deserted, businesses closed, shops empty. The mining camps spread into Queensland and Western Australia, where in the 1890s there was a famous gold strike at Kalgoorlie. The man who found the gold first, Paddy Hannan from Ireland, died broke.

Klondike
In 1897 two prospectors found gold in the Yukon River, in the far northwest of Canada. A gold town, Dawson City, grew up in less than a year. Ships carried miners from San Francisco to Skagway, and from there they trekked on foot or on horseback across the Chilkoot and White Horse passes. Then came an 800-kilometre riverboat journey to Dawson City as soon as the winter ice had melted.

The prospectors had to be tough. In winter the ground was hard with frost, and had to be thawed by lighting fires. Dawson was a noisy, rough community with dancehalls and bars. But some miners brought their wives, and there was a small clinic with four nurses.

South Africa
In 1886 gold was found at Witwatersrand in South Africa. Individual diggers rushed to the area but it was not long before they had been ousted by large mining companies, directed by a few rich men. By 1898 nearly 80,000 men were employed at Witwatersrand: 10,000 whites earning on average £26 per month, the rest blacks earning less than £3 per month.

Mining destroys the rain forest. Tracks become roads. Villages sprawl into *shanty* settlements. Disease is rife, for there is no proper sanitation. The local Indians lose their land and their lives are ruined. Fortunes are to be made. But very few of the poor miners drawn into the jungle by gold fever make them. The wealth goes into the pockets of the gold buyers, and the traders who sell basic necessities to the miners at exorbitant prices. Some miners never go home to their families. Those that do mostly return to the poverty that they left behind.

□ Official gold mines

South Africa produces two thirds of the world's gold and most of the world's diamonds. Huge resources are poured into the highly profitable mining industry. The mines employ hundreds of thousands of people and the latest extracting – and security – equipment. As well as gold, the mines yield valuable uranium.

Budie, California. Once miners swarmed over these bare hills. The wooden shacks were their homes. Today it is a ghost town.

Most of the miners that work in the mines are black. But they do not own them, or run them. Whites control the mines. South Africa's system of *apartheid,* or separation of the races, ensured that blacks did not become managers in the mines. This may soon change.

□ South African mining

Diamonds were found in South Africa in the 1870s and gold in the 1880s. Farms became mines overnight, with names now famous such as De Beers and Kimberley.

Boom towns sprang up as white miners flocked to the *diggings.* Black Africans were employed in the mines, hauling broken rock up the shaft in buckets tied to ropes.

Early on it became the rule that white miners gave the orders, while black miners obeyed them. The blacks came from farming communities and had no experience of mining techniques. They were, and still are, paid low wages, though many consider themselves more fortunate than those who work on farms, in domestic service, or have no jobs at all.

Discipline and security in the mines are strict. Workers are strip-searched on arrival and departure. Armed guards patrol inside and outside and there is constant closed-circuit television monitoring. There is no chance of any theft escaping attention.

An African family looking for diamonds. The simple cradle they are using to sift gravel is basically the same as the equipment used by the first South African diamond miners in the 1870s.

□ Away from home and homeland

Many of the workers in South Africa's gold and diamond mines are migrants. They come from the so-called homelands, or from neighbouring states such as Bots-

DIAMOND RUSH

In 1867 diamonds were found in the Orange and Vaal rivers in South Africa. Later they were found during dry diggings at a place called Kimberley. There was a brief free-for-all before powerful companies seized control of all mining activity. By 1891 De Beers Consolidated Mines controlled the whole diamond industry – and controls it to this day. Cecil Rhodes who went to South Africa for health reasons in 1871 was a major shareholder in the company. From it he derived the great fortune that still supplies money to fund the Rhodes Scholarships that he endowed.

wana – which also has its own mining industry. These workers live in drab *townships*, travelling to the mine by bus or train. They send money home to their families, whom they may not see for months.

□ Changing world

Diamonds are found in other African countries including Ghana, Namibia and Sierra Leone. The diamonds occur occasionally in river bed gravel or on the seashore. In Sierra Leone, thousands of miners prospect for diamonds illegally. They dig shallow *potholes* to get at the raw gems, which they sell without paying government taxes.

Black miners formed labour unions in South Africa to fight for better pay and safer working conditions. Many blacks can now match white miners in skills. As political change comes to South Africa and the system of apartheid breaks down, black miners will earn their rightful share of the industry's wealth. This will improve conditions for the migrant workers, and their families.

Miners drilling in a South African gold mine. South Africa has some of the deepest mines in the world.

1992

Nearly 100 years after the Klondike gold rush, Canada's isolated Northwest Territory is once again attracting prospectors – this time for diamonds which have been discovered in a wild, inaccessible region.

Mining Today and Tomorrow

A coal mining landscape. This is South Africa, but it could equally well be in Europe, North America or Asia. Smoke, steam, waste tips, looming pithead machinery: signs that human moles are at work.

In an effort to satisfy the world's demand for more and more stone, coal, metals, gems and phosphates, mining companies dig deeper and search further to reach new reserves. Despite mechanization, there will always be work for miners and money to be made from mining.

Communities that depend solely on the local mine are rare, but millions of people are employed in mining industries all over the world. The search for new minerals goes on. Prospectors no longer wander in the mountains with their belongings packed on the back of a mule. Instead geologists and geochemists survey likely areas from the air, using photographs taken by aircraft and space satellites.

When new mineral deposits are found, there is often a problem. Mines are not beautiful, but often the minerals are located in areas of outstanding beauty. The community then has to decide whether or not the mining company should be permitted to destroy the landscape. Nowadays when mine workings are abandoned, mining companies often dismantle the surface machinery and attempt to re-landscape the area. New techniques for growing plants on infertile *slag heaps* have been so successful that some coal tips now look as green as the surrounding countryside.

A valley in Wales. Sheep graze beside the pithead with its now disused winding gear and railway. One day the pit will be gone, the valley will be green again, and the community will enter a new era.

□ Dumping death and disease

Even worse than harming the landscape is the harm done to people and wildlife. In South America gold prospectors have poisoned rivers with the *mercury* they use to extract the gold. Abandoned tin diggings have become breeding grounds for disease-carrying mosquitoes. Indian communities are exploited, their land is taken and their health ruined by diseases such as measles brought in by the miners and farmers.

All over the world, unscrupulous mining companies dump waste materials into rivers and lakes, causing pollution and *ecological problems.*

□ Dust and noise

Mines cause air and noise pollution. People living nearby have to breathe in the smoke from the mine workings and furnaces, and from the dust caused by blasting. They also have to put up with the constant vibration that occurs in some mines and the noisy explosions that occur without warning.

In most western countries, there are strict regulations to control the mining companies' activities. In less developed parts of the world, where countries depend heavily on their mines for export income, controls are often less rigorously enforced.

Cutting coal underground by machine. The cutter works its way along the coal seam, cooling the face with water as it goes. It strips out the coal and automatically loads it on to a flexible steel conveyor.

□ Health and safety

The health and safety of workers are of concern to all but the worst mine owners, but standards vary from country to country. In western countries modern mines are clean and well ventilated. Fewer and fewer miners are disabled by diseases such as *pneumoconiosis, silicosis, asbestosis* and *emphysema* or poisoned by the dangerous metals that they mine. Fewer and fewer are injured by accidents at work – though more than 100,000 Americans have died in mining accidents this century. In less developed countries standards are lower, and preventable diseases and accidents frequently occur.

□ Old mines and new

No mine or quarry lasts forever. In the end they all become exhausted and the miners have to move on. When the high-grade iron ores of Michigan and Minnesota ran out, the mining companies began to extract iron from *taconite,* a low-grade ore that contains only specks and streaks of iron.

Tin was mined for 2000 years in Cornwall, but today the only tin mines are museums and the major industry of the region is tourism.

Modern strip-mines use gigantic machines to gouge out the coal and dispose of the waste.

When a mine is exhausted, or closed because it is uneconomic, people often feel bitter at the loss not just of their jobs, but of their traditions and community spirit. Elsewhere, however, new mines are opening and new communities taking shape.

□ Modern mines

The miner with pick and shovel has been replaced by machines: air hammers that break boulders, powerful drills that bore through the hardest rock, dredgers that suck up gravel from the bed of a river or ocean. Mountains of minerals are removed, altering the shape of a landscape for ever. Some mines are more than 3000 metres deep, with tunnels miles long. Modern mines are clean and airy, with fast-moving transport below ground.

The men and women who work in them now tend to be younger. As mines need smaller work forces, older men are given incentives to retire early, or in some places paid *redundancy money* when they are laid off.

In the next century, mining will be even more mechanized and computerized. But miners will still descend underground every working day. There will still be danger, from gas and dust, and worries for the miners' families. There will also still be that special feeling shared by those who work below ground.

POLLUTION

Mining and mineral- processing can cause serious environmental pollution. Mine workings scar the land, leaving heaps of waste. Some metals such as lead and mercury can poison soil and water. Waste from metal works may foul rivers and lakes. The heat and gases given off by burning coal and oil, and from smelting, add to the 'greenhouse effect'.

Glossary

Alloy A mixture of metals which makes for extra hardness or cheaper cost. Brass is an alloy of copper and zinc.
Amenities Facilities such as heating, sanitation, bathrooms and showers.
Apartheid Policy of racial separation enforced by the white government of South Africa until 1990s.
Asbestosis Disease affecting the lungs, caused by breathing in asbestos dust.
Bellpit Simple bell-shaped pit dug by early miners.
Blast furnace Used for making steel, by heating iron ore to high temperatures and blowing oxygen through it.
Boom town Town which grows rapidly as new settlers move in, for example, after a gold strike.
Cage Elevator, or lift, in a deep mine, worked by cables to lower miners down the shaft.
Charter Official document authorising the activities of an organization or business.
Claim Made by a miner to mark his ownership of a particular digging site. The area was marked out by posts or stakes – hence the phrase 'to stake a claim'.
Coke Fuel made by baking coal to get rid of the gases in it.
Colliers Coal miners. A colliery is another name for a coal mine.
Compensation Money paid to someone who has suffered loss or injury.
Conductor Substance that readily allows electricity to pass through it. Copper is a good conductor.
Conquistadors Conquerors; the Spaniards who captured the Aztec and Inca empires in the 1500s.
Deposit To lay or put down; a mineral deposit is a layer beneath the ground.
Developed nations Those with advanced industries and high standards of living.
Diggings Mines, usually shallow holes in the ground.
Ecological problems are those that affect the environment and upset the balance of nature.
Electroplating Process for adding a thin covering of one metal on another.
Emphysema Swelling of the lung causing breathing difficulties.
Explosives Chemicals such as gelignite and dynamite used for blasting in quarries and mines.
Export To sell goods abroad. Exports are the goods that a country sells abroad.
Flint Kind of stone that flakes and splits into pieces, used by Stone Age people to make tools.
Fossil fuels Fuels, such as coal and oil, formed millions of years ago from the remains of decayed plants and animals.
Galleries Tunnels leading off from a mine shaft.
Geochemist A person who studies the chemistry of the Earth's rocks.
Geologist A person who studies the history and development of the Earth through its rocks.
Ghost town Town deserted by its inhabitants when its main industry dies.
Gold strike First find of gold that sets off a gold rush.
Gunpowder The first widely used explosive, made from saltpetre, sulphur and charcoal.
Hewer Miner who cuts coal with a pickaxe.
High-tech A way of describing machines that use the latest technology.
Imports are goods that one country buys, or imports, from another.
Industrial Revolution: Period of rapid industrial development resulting from the introduction of machinery, particularly in Britain during 1700s and 1800s.
Ingot Solid block of pure metal.
Kiln Oven used to bake pottery and bricks.
Knocker-up Person who woke up miners early in the morning.
Labour Work, or the workers themselves.
Labour costs Wages and other costs of employing workers.
Mass-production Making goods cheaply in large numbers in factories.
Mechanization Use of machines to replace people's labour.
Mercury Metal unusual in being liquid at room temperature.
Minerals Any non-living substance such as rock or metal.
Nationalized industries are those controlled by the government rather than by private enterprise.
Nuclear power Power from splitting the atom.
Open-cast mine see *Strip mine*
Ores Rocks containing traces of metal.
Panning Using a metal pan to scoop up gravel that may contain bits of gold or other minerals.
Phosphates Minerals used to make fertilizers.
Pickaxe Mining tool used for hacking.
Picket Person who tries, on behalf of a trade union, to dissuade others from working during a strike.
Pit A deep shaft mine.
Pithead Buildings at the top of the mine shaft.
Pit ponies Horses used to draw

coal tubs or wagons underground.
Pneumoconiosis Chest ailment caused by dust.
Pollution The dirtying of the environment with poisonous or unpleasant substances.
Potholes Small quarries.
Prospect To search for minerals. A prospector is a person who searches for minerals.
Quarry Large hole dug to extract stone and other minerals.
Redundancy money is paid in some countries to workers who lose their jobs because the job no longer exists.
Reserves are deposits of minerals that remain to be mined.
Safety lamp Miner's lamp invented in early 1800s that prevented explosions caused by naked flames.
Seam Layer of coal sandwiched between other kinds of rock.
Shaft Vertical tunnel in a mine.
Shanty Roughly made hut.
Shift Work period in a mine or factory.
Silicosis Disease caused by breathing in silica (a mineral) dust.
Slag heap Pile of waste from a mine or quarry.
Sluicing A way of rinsing ore with water to wash away unwanted material.
Slurry Mixture of water, mud and rock.
Smelt To extract pure iron from iron ore by melting it.
Solidarity Comradeship, or determination to stick together in adversity.
Strike Withdrawal of labour by workers.
Strip mine, or open-cast mine, one where coal close to the surface is stripped away by machines.
Taconite Rock containing specks of iron oxide.
Tarnish To dull or discolour; some metals tarnish when exposed to oxygen or sulphur compounds.
Tokens Form of money paid to miners by some mine companies, to be spent at the company store.
Townships Small towns; especially those built to house black workers in South Africa.
Trapper Boy who used to open and close doors in an underground mine.
Unions Associations formed by workers to improve their working conditions and wages.
Uranium Metallic radioactive element used as fuel in nuclear power stations.
Ventilation Circulating fresh air through a mine.
Welfare insurance Government or private schemes to fund aid to sick or unemployed people.
Winding gear is the mechanism for hoisting and lowering the cage in an underground mine.

Index